NOW YOU CAN READ. . . .
ABRAHAM'S JOURNEYS

STORY RETOLD BY LEONARD MATTHEWS

ILLUSTRATED BY HARRY BISHOP

Library of Congress Cataloging in Publication Data

Matthews, Leonard.
  Abraham's journey.

  (Now you can read—Bible stories)
  Summary: Retells the Bible story of Abraham and his wife Sarah, to whom God gave a son named Isaac and the land of Canaan as a home for their descendants.
  1. Abraham (Biblical patriarch)—Juvenile literature.
2. Bible.   O.T.—Biography—Juvenile literature.
3. Bible stories, English—O.T. Genesis.   [1. Abraham (Biblical patriarch)   2. Bible stories—O.T.]
I. Title.   II. Series.
BS580.A3M35   1984   222'.11'0924   [B]   84-15130
ISBN 0-86625-313-0

Published by Rourke Publications, Inc., P.O. Box 3328, Vero Beach, Florida 32964. Copyright © 1984 by Rourke Publications, Inc. All copyrights reserved. No part of this book may be reproduced in any form without written permission from the publisher. Printed in the United States of America.
  The Publishers acknowledge permission from Brimax Books for the use of the name "Now You Can Read" and "Large Type For First Readers" which identify Brimax Now You Can Read series.

GROLIER ENTERPRISES CORP.

NOW YOU CAN READ....
ABRAHAM'S JOURNEYS

Long ago, a good man named Abram lived in a city called Ur. Many people lived in Ur. Some of these people did not believe in God. Abram did believe in God. One day he heard the voice of God. "Soon you must leave this country," God said. "Be ready. I will speak to you again."

Abram wondered why God spoke to him. Time passed. Again, Abram heard God's voice. This time God made some promises to Abram. "Leave this country," God said. "I will guide you to a new land. Do not be afraid. You are to be the father of a great nation."

"I will bless you and make your name great," God then said. Now Abram knew he had a special job to do for God. He told his wife, Sarai, and his nephew, Lot, what God had said. They gathered their servants and cattle and set out.

Day after day, week after week, they crossed mountains, plains and rivers. They kept moving southward. God guided them through the land of Canaan. Abram and his family settled in Egypt. There Abram became rich.

Abram had many herds of cattle and goats and many flocks of sheep. His nephew, Lot, became a rich man, too. Then God spoke to Abram again.

Egypt was not the country God wanted to give Abram. "You must leave Egypt," said God. At once Abram told Sarai what God had said to him. Sarai was sad to leave.

However, God had to be obeyed. So Abram and his family left Egypt. They went back to Canaan. The followers of Lot and Abram quarrelled. Abram was unhappy. "We must part," he told Lot. "You must go your way. I will go mine. Choose the way you want to go."

It was kind of Abram to allow Lot to choose first. Lot chose a green valley to the east where many rivers flowed. It was the best farming country. Lot, his family, his followers and his animals settled in the valley.

Abram, his family and his animals moved west. One day Abram heard the voice of God again.

"Look around you, Abram," God said. "Look to the north, to the south, to the east and to the west. This is my gift to you. All this land belongs to you and your people forever." Abram and Sarai set up their tent for the last time. They lived in the land of Canaan for the rest of their lives.

Many years passed. Abram was no longer a young man. Then one day he received bad news. His nephew Lot was in great danger. There lived at that time a cruel king. He was known as the King of Elam. He and his soldiers had attacked Lot and captured him and his family.

At once Abram called all his followers together. They set out and fought the King of Elam. Lot and his people were saved. How happy Lot must have been to see his uncle. Abram and his men returned home.

Abram had riches and land. Still, he was not happy. He and Sarai had never had children. This made them both sad.

Abram became old. He thought, "Sarai and I are now too old to have children."

God knew of Abram's sadness. So He made another promise to Abram. "You are the first of a great family," God said. "You and your wife will have a son. He will be named Isaac. You must change your name to Abraham. Abraham means 'the father of many.' Your wife Sarai must change her name, too. She will be called Sarah. Sarah means 'princess'."

Soon after this, Abraham was sitting
outside his tent. The day was hot.
Suddenly, three strangers appeared
as if from nowhere. Abraham smiled
in his friendly way. "Welcome to my
home," he greeted them.

Abraham pointed to a nearby tree. "It is too hot in the sun. Please sit there in the shade," he said.

Without saying a word, the three strangers sat in the cool shade.

Then Abraham called out to Sarah.
"These three travellers are hungry
and tired," he said.
"They need food."
Quickly Sarah
cooked some food.
She served it to the
three men.

The three men said nothing. They only nodded their heads as if to say "Thank you" and ate the meal. Abraham and Sarah stood together and watched the men. Abraham was sure they had not appeared just by chance.

One of the men seemed to be the leader. Finishing his meal, he spoke.

"Sarah will have a son," the man
said quietly. Abraham was very
surprised. How did the stranger
know Sarah's name? Sarah shook her
head and laughed sadly. "We are too
old to have children," she said.

When Sarah spoke, Abraham turned his head and looked at her.

When he turned toward the three men again, they had gone. It was as though they had never been there.

Soon a son was born to Sarah and Abraham. How wonderful! They called him Isaac which means "laughter." Abraham and Sarah were very happy at last. God had kept His word.

All these appear in the pages of the story. Can you find them?

the stranger

Lot

Abraham

Sarah

donkey

King of Elam

Now tell the story in your own words.